PRIMARY SCRIPTURES

Book of Mormon Stories for Kids

Volume 1 • 1 Nephi–Words of Mormon

This book belongs to:

_____

PRIMARY SCRIPTURES

Book of Mormon Stories for Kids

Volume 1 • 1 Nephi–Words of Mormon

Text adapted by Jason Zippro
Illustrated by Alycia Pace

© Primary Scriptures, LLC
All Rights Reserved.

No part of this book may be reproduced in any form whatsoever, whether by graphic, visual, electronic, film, microfilm, tape recording, or any other means, without the written consent of the author, except in the case of brief passages embodied in critical reviews or articles.

This is not an official publication of the Church of Jesus Christ of Latter-day Saints. The opinions and views expressed herein belong solely to the author and do not necessarily represent the opinions and views of the Church.

ISBN 13: 978-0-578-47044-3

REL046000 RELIGION / Christianity / Church of Jesus Christ of Latter-day Saints (Mormon)
REL091000 RELIGION / Christian Education / Children & Youth
JNF049200 JUVENILE NONFICTION / Religious / Christian / Early Readers

Cover design © 2019 Primary Scriptures, LLC
Illustrations by Alycia Pace
Cover design by Angela Baxter
Edited by Emily Chambers
Printed in South Korea

10 9 8 7 6 5 4 3 2 1

www.PrimaryScriptures.com

Contents

THE FIRST BOOK OF NEPHI ... 1

Lehi Sees a Vision of the Savior ... 3
1 NEPHI 1

Lehi's Family Leaves Jerusalem ... 8
1 NEPHI 2

Nephi Is Blessed by God ... 11
1 NEPHI 2

Nephi Is Obedient ... 15
1 NEPHI 3

Laban Keeps the Plates of Brass ... 19
1 NEPHI 3

Nephi Gets the Plates of Brass ... 25
1 NEPHI 4

Sariah and the Return of Her Sons ... 32
1 NEPHI 5

Ishmael and His Family Join Lehi ... 36
1 NEPHI 7

Lehi's Vision of the Tree of Life ... 43
1 NEPHI 8

Lehi's Testimony 1 NEPHI 10	56
Nephi Has a Vision 1 NEPHI 11-12	61
The Liahona 1 NEPHI 16	72
Nephi Breaks His Bow 1 NEPHI 16	76
Arrival to the Land Bountiful 1 NEPHI 17	82
Nephi Builds a Ship 1 NEPHI 17	85
Nephi Is Tied to the Ship 1 NEPHI 18	93
The Small and Large Plates of Nephi 1 NEPHI 9 & 19	99
Nephi Teaches His Brothers 1 NEPHI 20-22	102

THE SECOND BOOK OF NEPHI — 107

Lehi Teaches Jacob about Agency 2 NEPHI 2	109
Lehi Teaches Joseph about His Name 2 NEPHI 3	117

Lehi Blesses His Grandchildren and Dies 2 NEPHI 4	121
Nephites Separate from Lamanites 2 NEPHI 5	124
Jacob and the Gospel 2 NEPHI 9	131
Nephi Writes the Words of Isaiah 2 NEPHI 11	141
Isaiah Is Called as a Prophet 2 NEPHI 16	144
Isaiah Warns the People for Being Wicked 2 NEPHI 12, 13, 15 & 20	149
God's People Will Be Destroyed and Scattered 2 NEPHI 14, 15, 18	154
Isaiah Prophecies of Christ and the Last Days 2 NEPHI 12, 17, 19, 21	158
The Evil of Babylon Destroyed 2 NEPHI 23–24	163
Nephi Shares His Thoughts about Isaiah's Writings 2 NEPHI 25	169
Nephi Sees the End of His People 2 NEPHI 26	173
The Gospel of Christ 2 NEPHI 32	181

Nephi's Testimony 2 NEPHI 29–33	184

JACOB, ENOS, JAROM, OMNI, AND WORDS OF MORMON — 187

Nephi Dies JACOB 1	189
Jacob Warns of Sin JACOB 1-3	192
The Allegory of the Olive Tree JACOB 5	197
Sherem and Jacob JACOB 7	212
Enos Prays to God ENOS 1	219
Jarom and Omni Pass the Records Down JAROM & OMNI	225
The Words of Mormon WORDS OF MORMON & TITLE PAGE	233

NOTE TO PARENTS	241
REFERENCES	245
ABOUT THE AUTHOR & ILLUSTRATOR	247

The First Book of Nephi

Lehi Sees a Vision of the Savior
1 NEPHI 1

Lehi was a prophet of God. He and his family lived in the city Jerusalem.

One day, Lehi prayed for the people of his city. While he prayed, a pillar of fire came down on a rock in front of him. God showed him many things in the fire. The things Lehi saw made him shake.

Lehi grew very tired, so he returned home and fell asleep on his bed. While he slept, God showed Lehi more things in a vision. Lehi saw God sitting on His throne.

1 NEPHI 1

Lehi saw many angels singing about God. He watched as one angel, followed by twelve other angels, came and handed him a book to read.

Lehi read the book and felt the Spirit of God. Lehi shouted, "God and the things that He does are wonderful! God will help all His children!"

Lehi's Family Leaves Jerusalem
1 NEPHI 2

One night, God spoke to Lehi in a dream. God said, "You are blessed, Lehi, because you have obeyed me. Now, I have another commandment for you: You must take your family and go far away from Jerusalem."

1 NEPHI 2

When Lehi woke up, he obeyed God. Lehi and his family packed up many of their things. Then they left their home in Jerusalem.

After many days they set up their tents by a river near the Red Sea. Lehi took some stones and built an altar. Lehi prayed at the altar to thank God for their safety.

Nephi Is Blessed by God
1 NEPHI 2

Lehi had four sons: Laman, Lemuel, Sam, and Nephi. His youngest son, Nephi, was strong and loved God.

Nephi prayed to God. He wanted to know if all the things his father saw in his visions and dreams were true. God sent the Spirit to help Nephi know. The Spirit gave Nephi a warm feeling in his heart that meant the visions and dreams were true.

Nephi told his brothers what God had helped him learn. Sam believed what Nephi taught, but Laman and Lemuel did not believe Nephi.

Nephi prayed for Laman and Lemuel. After Nephi prayed, God said, "Nephi, you are blessed because you have faith and believe in me. If you keep my commandments, I will lead you to a promised land."

Nephi Is Obedient
1 NEPHI 3

Lehi had another dream. In this dream, God told Lehi to send his sons back to Jerusalem. They needed to get a special book of scripture called the Plates of Brass.

When Lehi told Laman and Lemuel what God had asked, they complained and whined. They did not want to go.

When Lehi told Nephi what God had asked, Nephi showed faith. Nephi said, "I will do what God has commanded. I know God won't command us to do something, unless He helps us do what He commanded."

1 NEPHI 3

After Nephi said this to his father, Lehi was very happy. Lehi knew that God had blessed Nephi.

Laban Keeps the Plates of Brass
1 NEPHI 3

Nephi and his brothers went back to Jerusalem for the Plates of Brass. They sent Nephi's older brother Laman to ask for the Plates of Brass from a wicked man named Laban. Laban did not like Laman. Laban called him a thief and sent him away.

Nephi and his brothers were sad Laman didn't get the plates. Nephi said, "We will not go back to our father Lehi until we have done what God has commanded. Let's go to our old home and get all our gold, silver, and expensive things. We can use them to buy the Plates of Brass from Laban."

So Nephi and his brothers brought their gold, silver, and expensive things to Laban. When Laban saw their riches, he became very greedy. Laban sent his servants after Nephi and his brothers to kill them.

Nephi and his brothers had to run away to save their lives. They had to leave all their gold, silver, and expensive things behind, so they could escape.

Laman and Lemuel were very angry with Nephi because they lost all their things. They were so angry that they got a pole and began hitting Sam and Nephi with it.

Then an angel came and stopped Laman and Lemuel from hitting Sam and Nephi. The angel asked, "Why do you hit your younger brothers with a pole? Don't you know that God has chosen Nephi to be your leader because you do not obey God's commandments? Go back to Jerusalem and God will help you with Laban."

Nephi Gets the Plates of Brass
1 NEPHI 4

Nephi said to his brothers, "Let's go back to Jerusalem and obey God's commandments. God is stronger than the whole earth, so He is stronger than all of Laban's servants. Don't you believe that we can get the Plates of Brass from Laban with God's help?"

Laman and Lemuel were still angry with Nephi, but they followed Nephi back to Jerusalem. Nephi had his brothers wait outside the city, while he snuck in at night.

Nephi didn't know what he needed to do. He followed the feelings of the Spirit. As Nephi got closer to Laban's house, he found Laban lying on the ground, motionless.

Nephi took Laban's sword and looked at how beautiful and well made it was. Then the Spirit told Nephi to kill Laban. Nephi didn't want to because he knew that God had commanded that we should not kill.

But the Spirit told Nephi again that God needed Nephi to kill Laban. The Spirit said Nephi's family needed the Plates of Brass. The plates had all the scriptures and commandments of God written in them.

Nephi obeyed. Then Nephi put on Laban's clothes and went to Laban's servant named Zoram. Nephi pretended to be Laban. He told Zoram to bring him the Plates of Brass and come with him.

Nephi led Zoram outside the city to Nephi's brothers. Nephi showed Zoram he wasn't Laban. He made Zoram promise to leave Jerusalem with them. So Zoram, Nephi, and his brothers journeyed back to Lehi and Sariah with the Plates of Brass.

Sariah and the Return of Her Sons
1 NEPHI 5

While Nephi and his brothers were away, their mother Sariah thought they had died. Sariah complained to Lehi, "You are a dreamer! You made us leave our home and brought us to the desert. My sons are gone, and we will die here in the desert too!"

Lehi tried to comfort her, "I know I see visions. Without my visions, I would not have known to leave Jerusalem. We would be destroyed like everyone else. Now, I know that God will protect our sons from Laban. God will bring our sons back to us."

1 NEPHI 5

When Nephi and his brothers returned, Sariah was very happy. She said, "Now I know God has commanded my husband Lehi to come to the desert. I know that God protected my sons!"

Lehi was so happy that he offered a sacrifice and a burnt offering to thank God. Then Lehi began to read the Plates of Brass. He wanted to know more about his ancestors and learn from the scriptures.

Ishmael and His Family Join Lehi
1 NEPHI 7

God commanded Lehi to send his sons to Jerusalem again. They needed to bring a man named Ishmael and his family back to the desert. So Nephi and his brothers went to get Ishmael and his family.

Ishmael obeyed God's commandment to go with Lehi's family. Ishmael's family took their things and left Jerusalem.

1 NEPHI 7

Laman, Lemuel, and some of Ishmael's children did not want to leave Jerusalem. They got angry with Nephi for making them leave.

Nephi said, "Laman and Lemuel, you are my older brothers. Why do I always have to be the good example for you? Don't you remember you've seen an angel? That God saved us from Laban and helped us get the Plates of Brass?"

Nephi's words made Laman and Lemuel very angry. They tied Nephi up and left him so wild animals could eat him. Nephi prayed for strength to escape. God answered his prayer.

When Laman and Lemuel saw that Nephi had escaped, they got even angrier. Ishmael's wife and children talked to Laman and Lemuel until they felt bad for tying Nephi up.

1 NEPHI 7

Laman and Lemuel asked Nephi to forgive them. Nephi quickly forgave them and told them they should pray and ask God to forgive them too. After Laman and Lemuel prayed, they all journeyed back to Lehi and Sariah.

Lehi's Vision of the Tree of Life
1 NEPHI 8

One night, Lehi had another dream. In the dream, Lehi saw a tree. The tree was covered in special, white fruit. Lehi ate some of the fruit, which was sweet and filled him with joy.

Lehi wanted his family to have some so they could feel the joy he felt. As he looked for them, he saw a river next to the tree. He looked far up the river until he saw his wife Sariah and two of his sons, Sam and Nephi.

He called to them. They came and ate some of the white fruit. Then Lehi saw Laman and Lemuel, but when he called to them, they did not want to come.

1 NEPHI 8

Lehi noticed that along the edge of the river was a small path. Along the path was an iron rod for people to hold on to. He also saw that the path and iron rod went all the way back past the beginning of the river into a very large field.

Lehi saw that the field was full of people. Some people began to follow the path toward the tree.

Soon a dark fog covered the field and path. Some of the people couldn't find their way anymore and got lost in the darkness.

Others grabbed the iron rod and followed it until they got to the tree and ate the fruit.

Across the river from the tree was a very large building. There were all kinds of people in it dressed in fancy clothes.

The people in the building were pointing at the people eating the white fruit of the tree. They were making fun of those eating the fruit and laughing at them.

1 NEPHI 8

Some of the people eating the fruit felt bad that the people in the building were laughing at them. They stopped eating the fruit and walked off into the dark fog and got lost.

But many of the people eating the fruit ignored the people in the building making fun of them. These people felt happy eating the fruit.

1 NEPHI 8

There were many people who went into the building. Others slipped and fell into the river. Others got lost in the darkness.

1 NEPHI 8

When Lehi woke from his dream, he told his family what he had seen. He was happy that Sam and Nephi listened and came to eat the fruit. He was sad and worried for Laman and Lemuel because they did not want to come.

Lehi's Testimony
1 NEPHI 10

Lehi shared his testimony with his family. Lehi said, "In 600 years, God will send a prophet to the Jews. This prophet will be Jesus Christ, the Savior of the world.

Another prophet will come before Jesus Christ. This prophet will preach to the people to prepare themselves for Christ's coming. His name will be John the Baptist.

1 NEPHI 10

John will baptize Jesus Christ and many other people. John will say he has baptized the Lamb of God, who will take away the sins of the world."

Lehi taught his children that the Jews won't believe Jesus. They will kill him. But after Jesus dies, He will return. He'll show Himself to people that aren't Jews, called Gentiles.

1 NEPHI 10

And Lehi shared many more things in his testimony to his family about Jesus Christ.

Nephi Has a Vision
1 NEPHI 11–12

Nephi was thinking deeply about Lehi's visions, when Nephi had a vision of his own. In the vision, Nephi was standing on the top of a mountain. The Spirit asked him, "What do you want?" Nephi said, "I want to see the things my father Lehi saw in his visions."

1 NEPHI 11–12

The Spirit asked, "Do you believe your father saw the tree with white fruit?" And Nephi said, "I believe everything my father has seen."

1 NEPHI 11–12

The Spirit shouted, "Hooray! Because you believe in God, you are blessed, Nephi. Now look!" Nephi looked and saw the tree with the white fruit. "What does it mean?" asked Nephi.

1 NEPHI 11–12

The Spirit showed Nephi the city of Nazareth. In the city there was a beautiful woman. The woman gave birth to a baby boy—Jesus Christ.

The Spirit also showed Nephi Jesus as an adult teaching many people.

1 NEPHI 11–12

The Spirit explained, "The iron rod is the word of God, which will always lead you to the tree. The tree is the Love of God."

1 NEPHI 11–12

The Spirit showed Nephi the baptism of Jesus, the Twelve Apostles of Jesus, and the death of Jesus.

1 NEPHI 11–12

Nephi then saw the building full of people from Lehi's vision. He saw it get destroyed. "The building is the pride of the world, and everyone who fights against God will be destroyed."

"Look!" the Spirit told Nephi. Nephi saw the promised land. There were many people angry with each other. The people battled against each other.

1 NEPHI 11–12

Then dark fog covered the land. There were earthquakes. There was lightning and fire. There were people scared and crying. The Spirit said, "the dark fog is the temptations of Satan. It confuses you to not believe in God."

1 NEPHI 11–12

Then Nephi saw the dark fog disappear. Jesus Christ came down from heaven and showed Himself to the people. Then the Spirit showed Nephi many more things that would happen in the promised land and the world.

The Liahona
1 NEPHI 16

While living by the Red Sea, Lehi had another dream. God told Lehi to keep traveling away from Jerusalem.

1 NEPHI 16

In the morning, Lehi went to leave his tent. By the door, he found an interesting brass ball.

Inside of the brass ball were two little pointers. They showed Lehi the direction he needed to go. The brass ball was called the Liahona.

So Lehi obeyed God's commandment. Lehi, Ishmael, and their families gathered their things and began traveling again.

Nephi Breaks His Bow
1 NEPHI 16

Lehi followed the directions of the Liahona. The Liahona helped the families find their way to places where there was food and water.

After many days of traveling, the families stopped to rest for awhile. Nephi took his steel bow and went to hunt for food. While Nephi was hunting, his bow broke.

1 NEPHI 16

His brothers were angry because they couldn't get any food without Nephi's bow. Everyone complained and whined because they were so hungry, even Lehi.

1 NEPHI 16

Nephi did not complain. Instead, Nephi decided to make a new bow and some arrows from wood.

1 NEPHI 16

When Nephi finished, he asked Lehi to ask God where he should hunt for food. Lehi prayed. God told Lehi that he should not have complained. Lehi felt very sorry. God showed Lehi with the Liahona where Nephi should hunt for food.

Nephi learned the Liahona only worked if everyone had faith and followed God's commandments written in it. He learned that God can use little things, like the Liahona, to make big and important things happen.

Arrival to the Land Bountiful
1 NEPHI 17

Nephi's family traveled for many years. They followed the Liahona and obeyed God's commandments from the Liahona.

Many things happened while they traveled. Ishmael grew old and died. Lehi and Sariah had two more sons, Jacob and Joseph. The families had many struggles. God always blessed them when they obeyed His commandments.

1 NEPHI 17

After eight years, the family arrived at a beautiful place by the ocean. This place was full of fruit, honey, and fresh water. The family stayed here and called the place Bountiful.

Nephi Builds a Ship
1 NEPHI 17

One day, God told Nephi to go up the nearby mountain. When Nephi got to the top of the mountain, he prayed to God. God commanded Nephi to build a ship. God showed Nephi how to build it.

1 NEPHI 17

God said the ship would take Nephi and his family across the ocean to a promised land. "I will be your light. I will guide you if you keep my commandments. When you arrive, you will know that I am God and that I have led you from Jerusalem to this new land."

So Nephi began to build the ship. As Nephi worked, Laman and Lemuel began to complain. They did not want to help build. They made fun of Nephi, saying that he was silly to think he could build a ship. They did not believe God had showed Nephi how to build a ship.

1 NEPHI 17

This made Nephi very sad. Nephi said to his brothers, "Don't you remember the story of Moses and how God helped them escape Egypt? God parted the Red Sea so they could escape. God also fed them with bread that fell from the sky and gave them water to drink from a rock!

1 NEPHI 17

God helped Moses and his people, like God helped our family escape from Jerusalem. You have been disobedient even though you have seen an angel. I am afraid that you will be destroyed because of the way you have both behaved."

1 NEPHI 17

When Laman and Lemuel heard what Nephi had said, they were angry and wanted to throw him in the ocean. They tried to grab Nephi.

Nephi said, "In the name of God, do not touch me! If you do, God will destroy you. Stop your complaining and help me build this ship. God commanded me to build it, and I will obey Him. I can do anything that God tells me to do."

1 NEPHI 17

God told Nephi to touch them. Nephi did, and God shocked Laman and Lemuel. Laman and Lemuel believed and began to help Nephi build the ship.

Nephi Is Tied to the Ship
1 NEPHI 18

Nephi finished building the ship. Everyone helped fill the ship with food, water, and things they would need. Then they set off for the promised land.

1 NEPHI 18

Laman, Lemuel, the sons of Ishmael, and their wives began to behave badly. They said very rude things. Nephi worried God would get angry, and he told them to stop.

1 NEPHI 18

Laman and Lemuel were angry, "We will not let our younger brother be our leader." And they took Nephi and tied him up.

As soon as they tied up Nephi, the Liahona stopped working. They didn't know where to steer the ship. Soon a great storm rocked the ship back and forth. They left Nephi tied to the ship for four days. The storm got worse and worse. They thought the ship would sink into the sea.

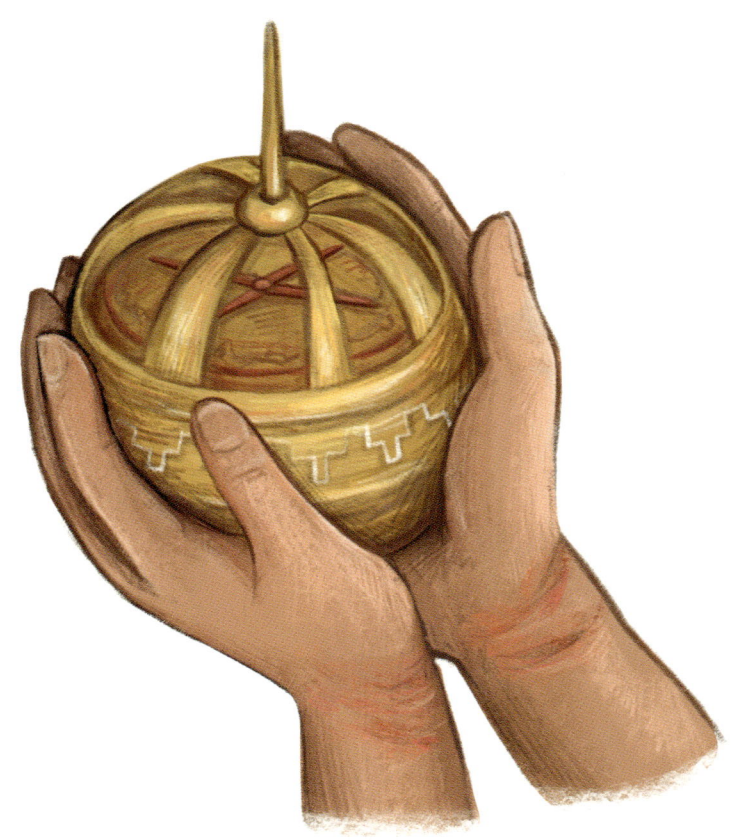

Laman and Lemuel were so afraid that they finally let Nephi go. Nephi's ankles and wrists were swollen, but Nephi did not complain. Nephi picked up the Liahona, and it began to work again.

Nephi prayed to God. The storm stopped, and the ocean was calm again. Nephi guided the ship for many days. Nephi and the families finally arrived in the promised land.

The Small and Large Plates of Nephi
1 NEPHI 9 & 19

God told Nephi to make a record. Nephi obeyed by making two sets of metal books called plates. He made a large set of plates and a small set of plates.

On the large plates, Nephi wrote down everything that happened to his family. He wrote about their journey from Jerusalem to the promised land.

1 NEPHI 9 & 19

On the small plates, Nephi wrote down spiritual things to help his people remember Jesus Christ.

Nephi Teaches His Brothers
1 NEPHI 20–22

Nephi wanted his brothers to always remember Jesus Christ. So, Nephi read from the scriptures to teach them. Nephi read the words of a prophet named Isaiah.

Nephi's brothers did not understand Isaiah. They asked Nephi to tell them what Isaiah's words meant. Nephi explained that God's people, the House of Israel, will spread out over the whole earth.

1 NEPHI 20–22

After Israel has spread out, God will create a great country. This country will be full of people, called Gentiles, who are not from the House of Israel.

1 NEPHI 20–22

In this great country, God will share His covenants and gospel with the people. God will then bring the House of Israel back to their homeland, and they will know Jesus Christ.

God will call a prophet and command us to listen and obey his words. Nephi told his brothers, "if we continue to obey God's commandments until the end of our lives, we will be saved."

The Second Book of Nephi

Lehi Teaches Jacob about Agency
2 NEPHI 2

Lehi grew old. He wanted to share his testimony with his children. He spoke to Jacob first. "Jacob, you are blessed because you have seen God's glory!"

2 NEPHI 2

In this life, everything has an opposite. There is good and evil, happiness and sadness. Some things can act, and other things are there to be acted on.

Without opposites, nothing would exist. But there is a God, and He created everything. God made us so we could choose and act for ourselves between opposites.

God even created Adam and Eve and the Garden of Eden. Adam and Eve had two opposite trees: the tree with the forbidden fruit and the tree of life.

2 NEPHI 2

Satan wants all of us to feel unhappy. He lied to Eve and told her to eat the forbidden fruit. After Adam and Eve ate the fruit, they had to leave the Garden of Eden. This was called the Fall.

The Fall let Adam and Eve have children. They could also now choose between good and evil. They could now feel happiness and sadness. Because of their choice, we all came to earth and will die someday.

Because of the Fall, we can all choose to be good or evil. If we choose good, we can live with Heavenly Father in heaven. If we choose evil, we will be unhappy and have to live with Satan.

2 NEPHI 2

Lehi finished his testimony by saying, "Remember to follow Christ and His commandments. Obey His words and listen to the Holy Ghost, so you can live with God in heaven forever!"

Lehi Teaches Joseph about His Name
2 NEPHI 3

Lehi also shared his testimony with his son Joseph and blessed him. Lehi said, "You are little, Joseph, but listen to your brother Nephi, and God will bless you.

2 NEPHI 3

Remember that we named you after one of our ancestors, Joseph of Egypt. Joseph saw visions of us and of the future. God promised Joseph that one of his grandchildren would be a mighty prophet like Moses.

This prophet will turn our records into a book of scripture. This prophet's name is also Joseph. Joseph Smith will take the book of scripture, which is the Book of Mormon, and teach from it.

God will also turn the Jewish records into a book of scripture called The Holy Bible. Both of these scriptures will teach people the truth. They will teach about God's covenants. They will help all people believe in Jesus Christ."

Lehi Blesses His Grandchildren and Dies
2 NEPHI 4

Lehi also blessed Laman and Lemuel's children. "I give you my blessing. If you keep God's commandments, He will bless you in the promised land. God will be kind to you and not let you be completely destroyed."

Then Lehi called Sam and blessed him. "Sam, you will do well in the promised land like your brother Nephi. God will bless your children like Nephi's children."

After Lehi gave his blessings, he grew older and died. After his father died, Nephi thought about his own life. Nephi was worried because of his sins. But Nephi loved God and was grateful to Him. Nephi trusted that God would help him be better.

Nephites Separate from Lamanites
2 NEPHI 5

After Lehi died, Laman and Lemuel grew more and more angry with Nephi. They didn't like their younger brother being their leader. They grew so angry that they decided to kill Nephi. They wanted to be the leaders.

God told Nephi to travel far away from Laman and Lemuel. So Nephi took everyone who would go with him. Zoram, Sam, Jacob, Joseph, and everyone else who believed in God left with Nephi. Nephi also took the Plates of Brass, Laban's sword, and the Liahona.

2 NEPHI 5

Everyone who left with Nephi called themselves Nephites. Everyone who stayed with Laman and Lemuel called themselves Lamanites.

The Nephites travelled for many days. When they stopped, they started to build a new city. They built farms, buildings, and even a temple. They worked hard. They learned to make things from wood and different metals.

Nephi worried the Lamanites would come attack the Nephites. So Nephi took the sword of Laban and made many swords like it. The Nephites could use the swords to protect themselves.

God warned Nephi. The Nephites should remember God and obey His commandments. If they didn't, God would let the Lamanites destroy them.

Nephi listened to God's warning and called Jacob and Joseph to be priests. Nephi told his younger brothers to teach the Nephites. So Jacob and Joseph taught the Nephites to remember God and obey His commandments. The Nephites listened and became a very happy people.

Jacob and the Gospel
2 NEPHI 9

As a priest, Jacob went around teaching the Nephites about God and Jesus Christ. Jacob taught the Nephites why Jesus Christ is so important to God's plan.

2 NEPHI 9

Jacob explained that everyone on earth makes mistakes. Sometimes we choose not to follow God's commandments. When we do things God doesn't want us to, it is called sin. We sin when we disobey His commandments.

2 NEPHI 9

Everyone sins sometimes. When we sin, it makes our spirits unclean. Only clean spirits can live with God. When we sin, we cannot go back to live with God without help.

Jesus Christ can help us be clean from sin. He is the only person who has never sinned. He helps us fix our mistakes when we sin, so we can return to live with God.

2 NEPHI 9

That is why Jesus Christ came to live on earth. He came to help us be clean from sin and to help us live with God again after we die. He can do these things because of the Atonement.

Christ suffered pain in the Garden of Gethsemane. His suffering for our sins is called the Atonement.

2 NEPHI 9

Christ was also hurt and died on the Cross of Calvary. But He came back to life. Because Christ died and came back to life, we can too.

2 NEPHI 9

When people die, their bodies and spirits separate. Resurrection is when a person's body and spirit come back together. Jesus Christ was the first person to be resurrected.

2 NEPHI 9

Jesus wants us to obey His commandments. Faith is when we trust Him enough to obey Him. He wants us to repent. Repenting means trying to fix our mistakes and do better next time when we sin. We also need to be baptized. Baptism is how we promise God that we will follow Him.

If we obey His commandments, have faith in Him, repent of our sins, and are baptized, then God will give us the gift of the Holy Ghost. The Holy Ghost will help us make good decisions. If we continue to obey His commandments for the rest of our lives we will return to live with God after we die.

Nephi Writes the Words of Isaiah
2 NEPHI 11

Nephi wrote in the small plates, "I have seen Christ and I love teaching my children that Christ will come again! Isaiah has also seen Christ, so I will write some of Isaiah's words."

HISTORICAL CONTEXT

In Isaiah's day, there were many of God's people. Some lived in Jerusalem like Isaiah. They were called the people of Judah, or the Jews. Others lived in Samaria. They were called the people of Ephraim, or the Israelites.

HISTORICAL CONTEXT

In those days, God's own people fought against each other. The Israelites fought the Jews. The Israelites brought another people, called the Syrians, to help them attack the Jews.

Isaiah Is Called as a Prophet
2 NEPHI 16

Isaiah was called to be a prophet. He had a vision where he saw God on a throne in the temple full of smoke. Angels stood by God. These angels had six wings. The wings meant they were very powerful. The angels glowed like they were on fire.

2 NEPHI 16

The angels shouted "Holy, holy, holy the God of Hosts, His light fills all the earth." Isaiah felt like he didn't belong because he wasn't perfect. But an angel put a hot coal on Isaiah's lips. This meant Isaiah's sins were forgiven.

God asked, "Who should I send to preach to the people?" Isaiah said, "Send me!" God warned Isaiah that many people wouldn't believe what he taught, even though Isaiah was a prophet.

HISTORICAL CONTEXT

Isaiah taught the people that there would be many wars because they weren't obeying God. He warned the people of Jerusalem that all God's people would be destroyed or taken as slaves.

HISTORICAL CONTEXT

The war between God's people in Isaiah's day is like the war between good and evil today. Isaiah wrote his words down to help us not be destroyed like his people were.

Isaiah Warns the People for Being Wicked
2 NEPHI 12, 13, 15 & 20

Isaiah tried to warn the people about sin. He said that God's people, the House of Israel, were very wicked. They only cared about their money and things, instead of God.

149

Isaiah warned about Satan. Satan is trying to destroy our families. He wants children to not listen to their parents. Satan wants the women of the church to only care about what they wear and how they look. But if they do, they will only feel lonely, embarrassed, and ashamed.

2 NEPHI 20 & 18

Isaiah told the people that God was unhappy with them. The people didn't take care of the poor and needy. Isaiah warned that anyone who doesn't help the poor and needy, won't get help or protection when they need it. God is like a rock that protects the righteous. But the wicked will trip over the rock.

Isaiah also told the people to watch out and be careful. There are people who will try to confuse you, even in the church. They try to make you think that bad is good, that darkness is light, and that bitter is sweet. These people help the guilty and punish the innocent.

2 NEPHI 13 & 15

Isaiah taught that Christ is the Bread of Life and the Living Water. If the members of the church aren't following Christ, their spirits will be hungry. Remember, when we don't obey God, we sin. Sinners are like an ox pulling a cart. Sins are heavy to carry.

God's People Will Be Destroyed and Scattered
2 NEPHI 14, 15, 18

In Isaiah's time, the King of Jerusalem was called Ahaz. Isaiah revealed to King Ahaz that a great enemy was coming. They were called Assyrians. They would destroy everything except Jerusalem.

2 NEPHI 14

Many of the men would be killed or taken as slaves. The women would be left without husbands. But God will comfort His people by giving them a temple as a safe place to go.

2 NEPHI 15

Isaiah told a story. "God had a growing vineyard on a hill. He protected it with a wall and a watchtower. He cleared out the rocks so the grapes could grow well.

God did everything He could to help the grapes grow. But they still grew bad grapes. So God said, "Let my vineyard be destroyed." Isaiah warned that the vineyard in this story is like the members of the church who don't repent. They are the wicked House of Israel.

Isaiah Prophecies of Christ and the Last Days
2 NEPHI 12, 17, 19, 21

Isaiah revealed more to King Ahaz. If King Ahaz obeyed God's warnings, Jerusalem's enemies would fail. As a sign that this was true, Jesus Christ would be born.

Isaiah continued, "For us this child is born. God's Son has been given to us. He will be our ruler. He will be called Wonderful Counselor, The Mighty God, The Everlasting Father, and The Prince of Peace."

2 NEPHI 21

Many years after Christ, Joseph Smith will live. He will have the Spirit help him. Joseph will begin to gather all of the House of Israel. Eventually, Jews and Israelites will no longer fight.

2 NEPHI 12

In the last days, the Temple of God will be built. Missionaries will go into the world to bring people to the temple.

2 NEPHI 12

When Christ comes again, there will be peace for many years. The people of the earth will take all their weapons and turn them into useful tools.

The Evil of Babylon Destroyed
2 NEPHI 23–24

There was an evil nation called Babylon. In the last days, Babylon is a symbol for evil. Isaiah taught that Zion, God's people, will gather and destroy Babylon.

2 NEPHI 23

God will lift a flag in the mountains to call His soldiers to battle. The soldiers are the members of His church. His soldiers will come from all over the world.

2 NEPHI 23

In the very last days, all people will feel afraid and guilty. The sun, moon, and stars will grow dark in the sky. The sinners will be destroyed. The earth and heaven will shake.

Once Babylon is destroyed, the survivors will be rarer than gold. Only hyenas and jackals will live in the empty, leftover buildings.

2 NEPHI 24

After Babylon falls, God's people will be glad. God will let them return to their own land and rest. They will say, "the whole world can now rest and be at peace. Sing for joy!"

The will also say, "Satan, who is the king of Babylon, fell from heaven. He tried to sit on God's throne, but he is now in darkness forever."

Nephi Shares His Thoughts about Isaiah's Writings
2 NEPHI 25

Nephi explained, "Isaiah's words will be important for the people in the last days. Prophets always warn the people before they are destroyed for their wickedness."

"The Jews did not listen to God, so they were destroyed. When Christ comes, the Jews will reject Him. They will crucify Him. They will put Him in a tomb. After three days though, Christ will rise from the dead."

"I have seen Christ's day! Everyone who believes in Christ will be saved in God's Kingdom. I saw that after Christ rises from the dead, Jerusalem will be destroyed again. The Jews will scatter over the whole earth."

"In the last days, God will gather His people again. He will bring them scriptures, so they will know who Jesus Christ is. I write about Christ so that my children and my people will believe in Jesus Christ. I want them to know who will forgive them of their sins."

Nephi Sees the End of His People
2 NEPHI 26

Nephi spoke more about Christ to his people. "After His resurrection, Christ will visit the Nephites to give us commandments."

2 NEPHI 26

Before He comes, prophets will show us signs to look for. These special signs will let us know when Christ is born. The signs will also let us know when He dies and is resurrected.

2 NEPHI 26

After Christ dies, there will be thunder and lightning. Many people will die in earthquakes and fire. All of the people in the promised land will suffer.

Everyone who believes the prophets will be protected. Everyone who obeys the prophets won't die. These people are called the believers. They watch for the signs even when others make fun of them.

2 NEPHI 26

After all the earthquakes and fires finish, Jesus Christ will come to visit. He will heal the people who are still alive. He will teach them how to have peace.

The people will become a kind and happy people for many years. The parents and children will live in peace. The grandchildren and great-grandchildren will also live in peace.

2 NEPHI 26

But the great-great-grandchildren will begin to not believe in Christ. They will not obey His commandments. These people will get worse and worse. They will fight each other and the Lamanites. They will fight until they are all destroyed.

Remember to follow God's commandments. Do not kill, lie, or steal. Do not swear using God's name. Do not hate someone because they have something you want. Do not hurt others or fight with each other. Do not love anything more than God.

The Gospel of Christ
2 NEPHI 32

"Remember that Jacob taught you to obey God's commandments," Nephi said. "Have faith in Jesus Christ. Repent of your sins. Be baptized. If you do these things, the Holy Ghost will help you.

2 NEPHI 32

The Holy Ghost speaks the words of Christ. The words of Christ tell you everything you should do. So read the scriptures because they are full of the words of Christ.

2 NEPHI 32

If you do not understand something, then pray to God and ask Him to help you understand. If you pray, God will help you understand by sending the Holy Ghost to teach you."

Nephi's Testimony
2 NEPHI 29–33

Nephi taught his people many things. When he was old, he shared his testimony with them. "Listen to everything I have taught you, and believe in Jesus Christ. If you don't believe in what I've taught, then at least believe in Jesus Christ.

2 NEPHI 29–33

If you believe in Jesus Christ, you will believe what I have taught you. Jesus Christ told me what to say and write, so these are His words. These words have taught you to do good.

2 NEPHI 29–33

God will show you that everything I have said are His words. He will show you that He commanded me to write them, and I obeyed Him. So listen and obey His words."

Jacob, Enos, Jarom, Omni, and Words of Mormon

Nephi Dies
JACOB 1

Nephi was growing too old to lead the people anymore. So, Nephi made someone king over the Nephites. The people loved Nephi because he was such a good leader. So, the people called the new king second Nephi so they would remember Nephi.

Nephi also kept the record of his people. He gave the record to Jacob. Nephi commanded Jacob to write down anything about Christ, about any visions he had, and anything that God told him to write. Jacob obeyed.

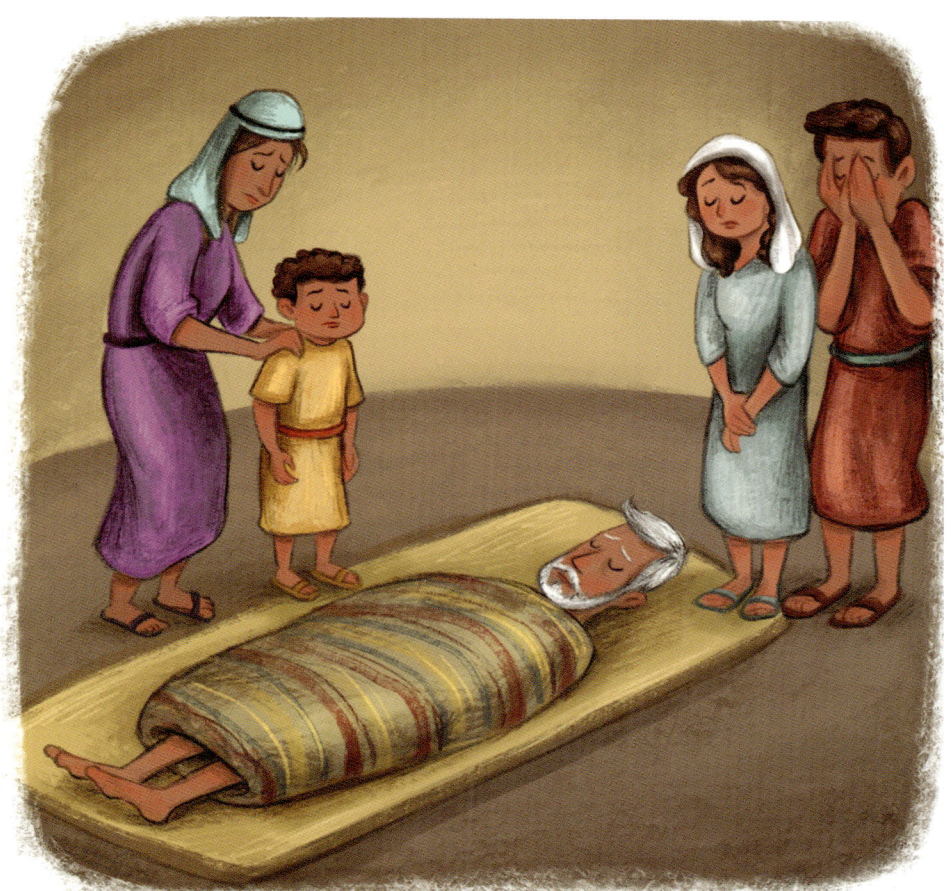

Soon, Nephi died. He had been a good ruler. He worked hard to protect his people from the Lamanites. He worked hard to help all his people be successful. He had taught them about Jesus Christ and His commandments. He taught them to obey God.

Jacob Warns of Sin
JACOB 1–3

After Nephi died, Jacob and Joseph went around and taught the Nephites to remember God. They taught the Nephites to believe in Christ and obey His commandments.

The Nephites began to sin. They didn't always obey God's commandments. They started to care more about money. They cared more about what others thought of them.

JACOB 1–3

Jacob went to the temple one day to teach the people. He said, "Nephites, you are beginning to sin. God told me to talk to you. And it makes me sad that I must tell you what you are doing wrong.

Many of you are beginning to care more about money. God has been good to you and given some of you more money than others. But you think you are better than others because you have more money than they do. God does not like this.

JACOB 1–3

Follow God's commandments. Use your money to help others who don't have as much as you. Give clothes to others who don't have any. Give food to others who don't have enough to eat. Help people who are in prison. Help others who are sick or sad."

The Allegory of the Olive Tree
JACOB 5

Jacob taught the people about the words of the prophet Zenos. Zenos spoke to God's people, called the House of Israel. "Pretend God's people are the branches of an old olive tree. This olive tree is in a large vineyard. Pretend the vineyard is the whole world."

God saw that His tree was beginning to get sick and die. So God tried to help the tree by giving it food and cleaning it up. When God calls a prophet, it is like feeding and cleaning up the tree. Prophets teach and warn God's people.

JACOB 5

A few good branches grew, but the tree was still sick and dying. So God cut off and burned the sick branches. The sick branches are the people who don't obey and follow God.

THE SCATTERING OF ANCIENT ISRAEL

God then cut off the few good branches and stuck them onto wild olive trees in the vineyard. God also cut off branches from the wild olive trees and stuck them onto the old, sick, dying tree. This means God scattered His people all over the world. This is called the Scattering of Israel.

Many days later, God and His servant checked on the trees. The wild olive branches made good olive fruit. The roots of the tree helped feed the branches, so they could grow healthy and strong. The roots are God's gospel and covenants. Covenants are promises we make with God.

JACOB 5

God looked at the good branches on the wild trees. They also grew good olive fruit, even though they were planted in poor soil.

JACOB 5

One wild tree was growing in good soil. It's olive fruits were both good and bad. God's servant said, "don't destroy it yet. Let's clean it up and feed it, and see if it will grow good olive fruit." These branches were the Nephites and Lamanites.

THE TIME OF CHRIST

Many days later, God and His servant checked on the trees again. All the olive fruit on the old tree were bad. God asked His servant, "What should we do? The roots are good. The roots don't help if the tree grows bad fruit though. And if we do nothing, the tree will die."

God went to check on the branches of the wild olive trees. All of them had also grown bad olive fruit. They checked the last tree that used to have both good and bad branches. They found that the good branch had completely died. All the Nephites and Lamanites were wicked.

THE GREAT APOSTASY

JACOB 5

God gathered the old olive tree branches that He put on the wild olive trees. He put them back onto the old olive tree. God also took the wild branches that He had put onto the old olive tree, and He put them back on the wild olive trees.

JACOB 5

God sent His servant to get all the other servants to come work in the vineyard. It was almost time to gather the good olives. The servants needed to help clean up and feed the trees so they would grow good olives one last time. This is the prophet calling all of us to be missionaries.

THE LATTER-DAY GATHERING OF ISRAEL

JACOB 5

The servants came and began to work. They cut off branches that were growing bad olives and burned them. With the bad branches gone, the branches growing good olives could grow better.

The servants worked long and hard. After awhile, the trees began to grow strong. They grew lots of good olives. God told His servants, "Bless you! You have listened and obeyed me. You have worked hard all this time to help the olive trees grow good olives."

THE LATTER-DAY GATHERING OF ISRAEL

JACOB 5

"Now," said God, "when bad fruit begins to grow on the trees again, I will gather all the good fruit. I will keep the good fruit safe. Then I will burn the whole vineyard. This will happen soon."

JACOB 5

"Remember to listen to and obey God and His servants, the prophets," Jacob explained. "We are the olives. As we obey God's commandments, we grow to be good. If we are good, God will gather and save us at the last day before He burns the rest of the world."

THE LATTER-DAY GATHERING OF ISRAEL

Sherem and Jacob
JACOB 7

Among the Nephites was a man named Sherem. Sherem started teaching the people that Jesus Christ would not come. Many people believed him because Sherem was very smart and good at speaking.

Sherem knew that Jacob believed in Christ. Sherem wanted to argue with Jacob because he wanted to make Jacob not believe in Jesus Christ. But Jacob had seen angels, and had even heard Christ speaking to him, so Sherem would not be successful.

Sherem spoke to Jacob, "You have been teaching people that Christ will someday come. You are lying because no one can know the future." Jacob replied, "Do you believe the scriptures?" Sherem said, "Yes."

Jacob replied, "All the prophets in the scriptures have written about Christ. And the Holy Ghost has told me that Christ will someday come." "If that's true," said Sherem, "then show me a sign to prove that this Holy Ghost is real."

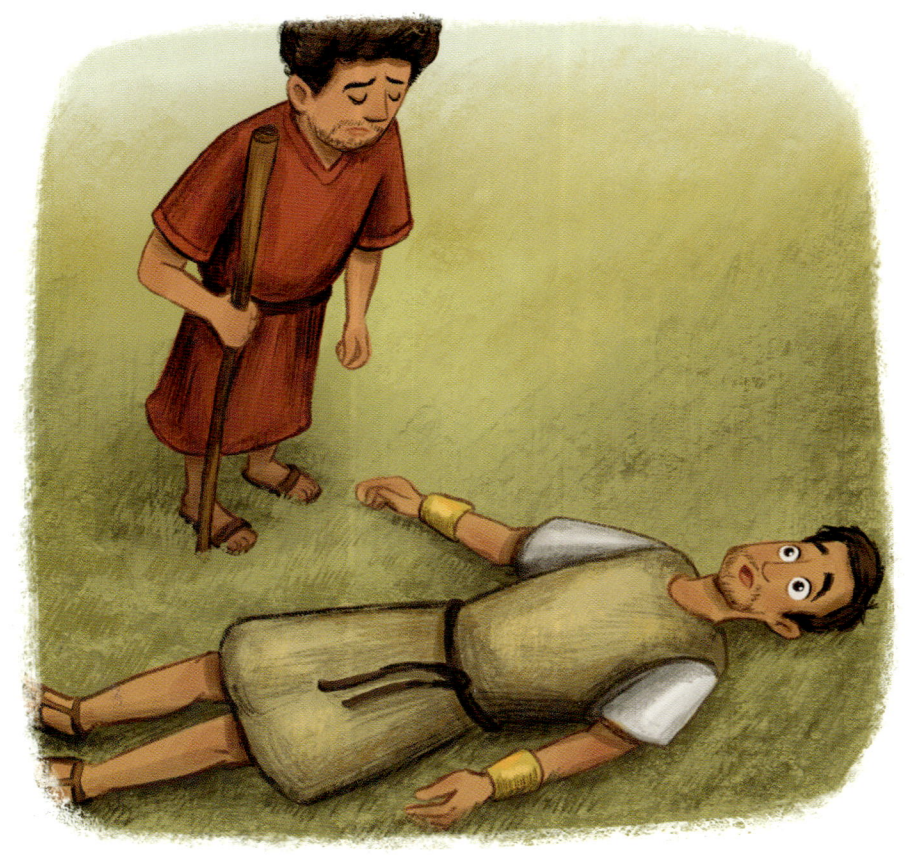

Jacob said, "If God wants to show you a sign, then let Him make you weak and fall down. But it is God's choice if He will show you a sign." Sherem immediately fell down. It took many days before he was strong enough to speak to the Nephites.

Sherem explained, "I have been tricked by Satan. Everything I have told you is a lie. Christ will come, and the Holy Ghost and angels are real. I am sad because I know God is very unhappy with what I did. I hope He forgives me." Then Sherem died.

The Nephites were amazed. They began to read the scriptures again and believe in Christ. And they began to send missionaries to teach the Lamanites about Christ.

Enos Prays to God
ENOS 1

Enos was Jacob's son. One day, Enos was in the forest hunting wild beasts, when he remembered some of his father's teachings.

Enos wanted to know if God would forgive his sins, so he knelt down and began to pray. Enos prayed all day without stopping. When night came, Enos was still praying.

While Enos was praying, God spoke to Enos. "You are blessed. Your sins are forgiven because you have faith in Christ."

When Enos heard these words, he thought about the Nephites. So Enos began to pray for the Nephites. God told Enos that if the Nephites kept God's commandments, He would visit them.

When Enos heard God's promise, he started to pray for the Lamanites. God promised Enos that God would bless the Lamanites too.

Enos learned the power of prayer. He learned that if you ask God for something good, He will give it to you, if you believe in Jesus Christ.

Jarom and Omni Pass the Records Down
JAROM & OMNI

Now the record passed down from Jacob to Enos to his son Jarom. In Jarom's days the Nephites were good. Because they kept the commandments, God blessed them to be rich and strong. God protected them from the Lamanites.

JAROM & OMNI

Jarom gave the records to Omni, his son. And the records got passed down again and again for over three hundred years. From Omni to Amaron. Then to Amaron's brother Chemish. Then Chemish gave them to his son Abinadom. And Abinadom gave them to his son Amaleki.

JAROM & OMNI

In Amaleki's days, there was a king called Mosiah. God spoke to King Mosiah and told him to take the Nephites and leave their cities. King Mosiah obeyed.

JAROM & OMNI

King Mosiah and the Nephites travelled far away from the land of Nephi. They came to a city called Zarahemla.

JAROM & OMNI

Like Lehi, the people of Zarahemla had also come from Jerusalem. God led them to the promised land too. But they had forgotten God, because they didn't have scriptures with them.

JAROM & OMNI

When Lehi and his family left Jerusalem, God sent Nephi and his brothers back to get the Plates of Brass. The plates had the scriptures in it so they could remember the commandments of God.

The Nephites stayed in Zarahemla. The people of Zarahemla made King Mosiah their king too. Now the people of Zarahemla and the Nephites were all called Nephites. After many years, King Mosiah's son Benjamin became King.

Amaleki, who had the records, didn't have any children to give his records to. So Amaleki gave them to King Benjamin. Benjamin was a good king who obeyed God's commandments.

The Words of Mormon
WORDS OF MORMON & TITLE PAGE

Many years after King Benjamin, there was a prophet named Mormon. In Mormon's day, all the Nephites died. They died because they no longer listened to God or obeyed His commandments.

WORDS OF MORMON & TITLE PAGE

Mormon received all the Nephite records. He had the Plates of Brass. He had the records Nephi and Jacob kept, the Small Plates of Nephi. He had the Large Plates of Nephi written by the kings of the Nephites. And he had many other records too.

WORDS OF MORMON & TITLE PAGE

God commanded Mormon to rewrite the Nephite records onto small, golden pages. These pages are the Gold Plates.

WORDS OF MORMON & TITLE PAGE

Joseph Smith was given the Gold Plates. The angel Moroni showed Joseph where to find them. Joseph translated the words from the Gold Plates. Joseph's translation is The Book of Mormon.

WORDS OF MORMON & TITLE PAGE

The Book of Mormon teaches us the great things God has done for His people. The Book of Mormon helps us remember the promises we made with God and God's commandments.

WORDS OF MORMON & TITLE PAGE

The Book of Mormon was written so all God's children would believe in Jesus Christ.

Note to Parents

PURPOSE

The goal of this book is to engage young children in the stories of the Book of Mormon. It is not meant to replace your reading and study of the actual text of the Book of Mormon. It is my hope that as you use this book in Family Home Evening lessons, as a resource in your family scripture studies, or just as a bedtime storybook, that it will spark gospel discussions between you and your child. Ultimately, I hope that this book will help you and your child strengthen your testimonies of Christ as the Savior and Redeemer of all humankind.

CONSTRAINTS

Adapting the Book of Mormon text into simpler language means that many of the details and nuances from the stories had to be left out. Additionally, retelling the stories was my primary intent, not interpreting the doctrines contained in the Book of Mormon. However, it is impossible, nor the intent of this book, to completely decouple the stories from the doctrines they illustrate.

NOTE TO PARENTS

So, where I do address doctrines, I try to focus on the most foundational doctrines, such as the gospel of Jesus Christ, and I try to strictly adhere to the interpretations of the scriptures as written in Church-published materials. (See the end of this note for a complete list of publications referenced during this project.)

INTERPRETIVE CHOICES

There are two sections in this first volume where I decided to deviate from the normal pattern of the narrative.

The first departure is my interpretation of 2 Nephi 9 entitled in this volume as "Jacob and the Gospel." For this story, I chose to address key gospel principles that are not actually addressed in 2 Nephi 9 of the Book of Mormon. To be clear, all of the doctrines I do address are taught throughout the Book of Mormon, but in order to make the gospel principles taught in a cohesive way, I decided to consolidate them here in this one story. The ultimate goal is that the principles of the gospel of Jesus Christ will be more understandable when all shared in relation to each other.

The second departure occurs in the Isaiah chapters in 2 Nephi. Due to Isaiah's prolific use of repetition

NOTE TO PARENTS

(specifically chiasmic patterns), extensive motifs, and metaphors, I had to make several organizational and interpretive choices that hopefully will help clarify some of Isaiah's warnings and prophecies for the latter-days. The referenced chapters are not necessarily sequential in this section. Additionally, many of Isaiah's teachings are not included; however, I did try to address the major themes and key teachings of those chapters. These included Isaiah's call as a prophet, the scattering and gathering of Israel, and his prophecies of the last days.

All of my interpretations of Isaiah's words were primarily taken from the Church's institute manual on the Book of Mormon and general conference talks given by current and former apostles and prophets (accessed through scriptures.byu.edu).

Additionally, portions of these stories are not included in the scriptures at all, but are rather descriptions of the historical context in which Isaiah lived, to better help explain the context of Isaiah's words. For these sections, I primarily referenced a book entitled *Isaiah: Prophet, Seer, and Poet* written by Brigham Young University's foremost scholar on Isaiah, Victor Ludlow.

NOTE TO PARENTS

ENDING THOUGHTS

Finally, I would like to say that this whole project began as a way for me to help my own children understand the stories and gospel principles of the Book of Mormon. It has been inspiring as I have written and rewritten these stories to hear my own children understanding key gospel topics and likening the scripture stories to themselves and their everyday lives. It is my hope that reading this book will spark similar gospel discussions in your own home and, ultimately, strengthen your children's testimonies.

References

1. *The Book of Mormon: Another Testament of Jesus Christ.* Salt Lake City: The Church of Jesus Christ of Latter-day Saints, 1981.
2. *Book of Mormon Student Manual: Religion 121–122.* Salt Lake City: The Church of Jesus Christ of Latter-day Saints, 2009.
3. *Gospel Principles.* Salt Lake City: The Church of Jesus Christ of Latter-day Saints, 2009.
4. James Strong. *The New Strong's Expanded Exhaustive Concordance of the Bible.* Nashville: Thomas Nelson, 2001.
5. *Preach My Gospel.* Salt Lake City: The Church of Jesus Christ of Latter-day Saints, 2004.
6. *True to the Faith.* Salt Lake City: The Church of Jesus Christ of Latter-day Saints, 2004.
7. Victor L. Ludlow. *Isaiah: Prophet, Seer, and Poet.* Salt Lake City: Deseret Book, 1982.

About the Author and Illustrator

AUTHOR

Jason Zippro holds a master's degree in education from the University of Missouri-Saint Louis, a master's degree in business administration from the University of Utah, and a bachelor of arts degree in Italian with a minor in editing from Brigham Young University. Jason worked as an editor for four years before teaching 8th grade English for three years in Kansas City with the non-profit Teach for America. Jason and his wife, Sharolee, have four children ages 1–6.

ILLUSTRATOR

Alycia Pace graduated from Brigham Young University with a bachelor of fine arts degree in animation and is a freelance illustrator from her home in Utah. She has written and illustrated several books including *Polly the Perfectly Polite Pig* (available at Deseret Book and Barnes & Noble) and soon to be available, *How to Train a Dinosaur to Use the Potty*. She loves the smell of bookstores and exploring new places with her two children and adventurous husband.